You Are...

VOLUME ONE

Lauren Brownrigg

TULSA

ISBN: 978-1-957262-38-3 HC
978-1-957262-39-0 PB
You Are ...: Volume One

Yorkshire Publishing
1425 E 41st Pl
Tulsa, OK 74105
www.YorkshirePublishing.com
918.394.2665

Published in the USA

CONTENTS

You Are ... Loved

"In all the world, there is no heart for me like yours.
/ In all the world, there is no love for you like mine".

- Maya Angelou, Soul Shattering Poetry

When I say "You are loved," what does it mean?
It is a word, a feeling, a reason for being.
To love someone is an incredible thing,
It makes your spirit soar and your heart sing.

It is shown through our words, but also our actions
through our smiles, tears, or other reactions.
It is built every day by the memories we share,
In the way that we show each other we care.

Love means I am full of warmth and affection for you,

You fill my life with joy and hope in all that you do.

I will be there for you when you are happy or sad,

the choices you make, the good or the bad.

Protecting you the best way that I can,

Even when that means saying no and disrupting your plan.

Loving you means that I will always do my best,
To show you you're important and support you on your quest.
Ready with open arms whenever you need,
an embrace of protection or someone to take the lead.

Love grants me the honor and privilege to be

A guardian, a keeper, a protector of thee.

Giving me a glimpse of what God may see,

When he looks down upon the child in me.

You are a precious gift, made perfect for my heart,
An unconditional love created from the start.
Love will hold us together like an invisible bond,
in this life on Earth and forever beyond.

When I lay you down tonight I pray you never have to doubt,

what the meaning of love is truly about.

My love will remain as sure as the setting sun,

And I will remind you each time the day is done…

You are … loved

Definition:

Love: (noun)

a feeling of strong or constant affection for a person

Discussion:

Who are some people that you love? What do you do to make them feel loved? What have they done for you that makes you feel loved? Think back on your day; have you done anything that showed love to someone else? How did it make you feel? How did it make the other person feel?

Use the journal page to write a memory about a time you showed or received love, or about someone you love and care about.

_____
_____
_____
_____
_____
_____
_____
_____
_____
_____
_____
_____
_____
_____
_____
_____
_____
_____
_____
_____
_____

Look back at this memory and feel the love you have for these people, or the love in this moment.

Never forget how much you are…loved.

You Are ... Enough

"I have always been enough, simply by being. Simply by being here, as I am". —Jennifer Williamson, Healing Brave

When I say "You are enough," what does that mean?
It means that what you have to give is all that's required,
Just the way you are is forever desired.

When you were born I prayed over you,

that each day you lived you saw all you could do.

Hoping you'd realize the potential I see,

and all the wonderful things you could be.

Teaching you to work hard and have confidence,

pushing yourself to go the distance.

I'll be there to help when you feel down,
knowing some days you might come home with a frown.
Hurting to see you think less of yourself,
watching you want to put your dreams on the shelf.

I'm here to remind you that there is no one like you,
and that you are enough in all that you do.

You don't need to push yourself until you can't do anymore,
there is no one but you keeping score.
Keep trying hard and doing your best,
do not listen to all the rest.

Be proud of yourself and share your shining light,
reaching for the goal just out of sight.
In the eyes of those that love you, remember what we see,
we see someone special, someone young, and free.

Never believe the world's harmful bluff,
love yourself and remember

You are ... enough.

Definition:

Enough: adjective

Equal to what is needed

Discussion:

There are times in life that you may not feel like you are doing things good enough. To your family and friends, you will always be enough, just the way you are. Think of a time when you felt important and like you were doing things right. How did it make you feel? Did you feel like you were enough in that moment?

Use the journal page to write down this memory, or another memory of a time when you felt like you gave all that was needed and you were enough.

_____
_____
_____
_____
_____
_____
_____
_____
_____
_____
_____
_____
_____
_____
_____
_____
_____
_____
_____
_____
_____

If you ever have a time when you begin to doubt yourself and all your capable of, look back at this memory and remember you are…enough.

You Are ... Kind

"In a world where you can be anything, be kind." - unknown

When I say "You are kind," what does it mean?

It means you are loving and tender, and so much in between.

As you grow up I see who you'll become,

someone who will never make another feel unwelcome.

Loving those around you with smiles and joy,

no matter who they are, girl or boy.

Truly a gift to each friend you make,
never meeting a stranger or appearing fake.
Seeing each person for the things they do best,
not paying attention to all the rest.

Making sure each friend had a place in line,

Or reaching out to make sure they were fine.

Feelingly strongly for those you love,

praying for them to the Father above.

Living life by the Golden Rule,
never looking at others as though they were the fool.
Using your manners and being polite,
knowing in your heart it's what's right.

I see you wear your heart on your sleeve,
hoping this quality will never leave.

As you grow up I pray you know what's on my mind, that to me you are precious, and

You are … kind

Definition:

Kind: adjective

having or showing a gentle nature and a desire to help others: wanting and liking to do good things and to bring happiness to others

Discussion:

Look back on your day and think of a time when you were kind, or someone was kind to you. What did you do to be kind? What did they do to be kind? How did it make you feel? How did it make them feel?

Use the page below to write down this memory, or another memory of a time you were kind or someone was kind to you.

_____

_____

_____

_____

_____

_____

_____

_____

_____

_____

_____

_____

_____

_____

_____

_____

Anytime you need a reminder of how to be kind, look back and remember you are…kind!

You Are ... Remembered

"I carry your heart with me (I carry it in my heart)" – E. E. Cummings

When I say "You are remembered," what does it mean?

It is a memory, a moment, a loved one unseen.

Someone who holds a precious place in your heart,

Even though you may be apart.

It could be someone you know that you loved so dear,
Someone who's voice you long to hear.
It could be someone you never had the chance to meet,
A piece of your life that feels incomplete.

It could be a pet, who never left your side,

Who's trust was unwavering, a safe place to confide.

The pain of missing them may never go away,

But the love you have for each other will always stay.

Although you can't see them they are never very far,

For they live in your heart and wherever you are.

Each blessing you receive is a sign you will see them again,

giving permission for the healing to begin.

You can remember the good times or the times you wished you had,

and every now and then remember it's okay to be sad.

Take comfort in knowing they are shining beyond heaven's gate,

and that they will always be watching over you, guiding your fate.

Someday you will reunite, and what a reunion it will be,

The greatest of parties, a magnificent sight to see.

Until that day comes think of them each day,

and in your heart let them hear you say…

You are … remembered.

Definition:

Remembered: verb

to have or keep an image or idea in your mind of (something or someone from the past) : to think of (something or someone from the past) again

Discussion:

Losing someone is very hard, and grief is a feeling that takes time to go away. The sadness we feel is a reminder that they were important to us and that we loved them very much. Who are some loved ones that you miss today? How do you feel when you think about them? What are some of your favorite memories with them?

Use the page below to write down a list of people you love and remember and what you remember most about them.

_____

_____

_____

_____

_____

_____

_____

_____

_____

_____

_____

_____

_____

_____

_____

_____

_____

_____

On the days when the sadness becomes too much, look at these names and memories, and remember they are with you wherever you go.

Think of them and tell them, you are…remembered.

CPSIA information can be obtained
at www.ICGtesting.com
Printed in the USA
BVHW021116260822
645501BV00025B/246

9 781957 262383